Franz Keibel

Normentafeln zur Entwicklungsgeschichte der Wirbeltiere

Band 10

Franz Keibel

Normentafeln zur Entwicklungsgeschichte der Wirbeltiere
Band 10

ISBN/EAN: 9783743322912

Hergestellt in Europa, USA, Kanada, Australien, Japan

Cover: Foto ©berggeist007 / pixelio.de

Manufactured and distributed by brebook publishing software (www.brebook.com)

Franz Keibel

Normentafeln zur Entwicklungsgeschichte der Wirbeltiere

NORMENTAFELN
ZUR
ENTWICKLUNGSGESCHICHTE DER WIRBELTIERE.

IN VERBINDUNG MIT

Dr. BLES-Glasgow, Dr. BOEKE-Helder, Holland, Prof. Dr. BRACHET-Brüssel, Prof. Dr. B. DEAN-Columbia University, New York, U. S. A., Dr. H. FUCHS-Strassburg, Dr. GLAESSNER-Strassburg, Prof. Dr. O. GROSSER-Wien, Prof. Dr. R. HENNEBERG-Giessen, Prof. Dr. HUBRECHT-Utrecht, Prof. J. GRAHAM KERR-Glasgow, Prof. Dr. KOPSCH-Berlin, Dr. THILO KRUMBACH-Breslau, Prof. Dr. LUBOSCH-Jena, Prof. Dr. P. MARTIN-Giessen, Dr. NIERSTRASZ-Utrecht, Prof. Dr. C. S. MINOT-Boston, U. S. A., Prof. MITSUKURI-Tokio, Prof. Dr. NICOLAS-Paris, Prof. Dr. PETER-Greifswald, Prof. REIGHARD-Ann Arbor, U. S. A., Dr. SAKURAI-Fukuoka, Japan, Dr. SCAMMON-Harvard Medical School, Boston, U. S. A., Prof. Dr. SEMON-Prinz-Ludwigshöhe bei München, Prof. Dr. SPULTA-Würzburg, Prof. Dr. SOULIE-Toulouse, Prof. Dr. TANDLER-Wien, Dr. TAYLOR-Philadelphia, U. S. A., Prof. Dr. TOURNEUX-Toulouse, Dr. VOELKER-Prag, Prof. WHITMAN-Chikago, U. S. A.

HERAUSGEGEBEN VON

Prof. Dr. F. KEIBEL, LL. D. (HARVARD),
FREIBURG I. BR.

ZEHNTES HEFT.
NORMAL PLATES OF THE DEVELOPMENT OF LEPIDOSIREN PARADOXA AND PROTOPTERUS ANNECTENS.

BY

J. GRAHAM KERR
UNIVERSITY OF GLASGOW.

WITH 1 FIGURE IN THE TEXT.
AND 3 PLATES.

JENA,
VERLAG VON GUSTAV FISCHER.
1909.

Alle Rechte vorbehalten.

Contents.

Introduction
General Sketch of the Course of Development in *Lepidosiren* and *Protopterus*
    External features
    The skin
    Nervous system
    Peripheral nerves
    Olfactory organ
    Eye
    Otocyst
    Skin sense organs
    Pinkus' organ
    Pituitary body
    Alimentary canal
    Buccal cavity
    Visceral clefts
    Lung
    Thyroid and thymus
    Digestive tract
    Liver
    Pancreas
    Coelomic organs
    Splanchnocoele
    Myotomes
    Nephridial system
    Archinephric ducts
    Mesonephros
    Genital ducts
    Gonads
    Organs of the mesenchyme
    Skeleton
Tables
Conclusion
Literature

Introduction.

In selecting the various "stages" which were to form the basis of my work upon the development of *Lepidosiren* and *Protopterus* I realized from the beginning the importance of making my series of "stages" agree as closely as possible with the series of stages defined by SEMON in his classical work on *Ceratodus*. In would clearly have greatly facilitated the comparison of data obtained from the investigation of the development of the Monopneumona and Dipneumona and therefore have added to the value of these data if the developmental history could have been divided into exactly corresponding stages. A little investigation was sufficient to make clear the impossibility of arranging any such corresponding series of stages and I was therefore compelled to make my selection of stages of *Lepidosiren* quite independent of those selected by SEMON for *Ceratodus*. In defining the stages of *Protopterus* I have endeavoured to make them correspond in number with those of *Lepidosiren* but even here it will be seen that the agreement between the stages of *Lepidosiren* and *Protopterus*, although the two genera are so closely allied, is only of a comparatively rough kind, and I have had to make the descriptive tables quite independent. The figures reproduced in the three plates cover the developmental history of the two genera fairly completely up to stage 36, except that in the case of *Protopterus* the early stages of segmentation have not yet been observed. I have not thought it advisable to include figures of stages subsequent to 36, when the adult form is being assumed, as their inclusion in the plates available would have necessitated the reduction in size of the earlier and more important figures.

For the figures of the various stages I am indebted to the high artistic skill combined with conscientious care of Mr. A. K. MAXWELL. They have been drawn throughout under my close supervision and I can vouch for their accuracy. The necessary section cutting has been carried out with his usual skill and care by Mr. P. JAMIESON.

The data given in the Tables are to be taken as referring to the specimens figured. In most cases several, in some cases numerous, specimens belonging to the same stage according to their external features have been investigated by sections and in the few cases where it has seemed necessary to include data derived from such other specimens such data are enclosed between brackets. Such necessity has arisen in various cases where particular points can be determined with greater accuracy in sections cut in different planes from those in which the specimen figured had been cut or prepared by different embedding or staining methods.

Seeing that the present part of the "Normentafeln" deals with forms so little familiar to embryologists generally I have thought it advisable to preface the Tables with a short sketch of the general development of the two forms in question.

General Sketch of the Course of Development in Lepidosiren and Protopterus.

External features. (*Lepidosiren*, GRAHAM KERR, 1900a; *Protopterus*, BUDGETT, 1901.)

The egg of *Lepidosiren* (6,5—7 mm) and that of *Protopterus* (3,5—4 mm) undergo a complete but unequal segmentation. In *Lepidosiren* the first two furrows are meridional and they are succeeded by a series of four vertical furrows. These are liable to variation and individual furrows may become actually latitudinal. In the case of *Protopterus* the early phases in segmentation have not yet been observed.

Segmentation results in the formation of a blastula with a large segmentation cavity, roofed in by two layers of micromeres and overlying the heavily yolked macromeres which form the lower part of the egg. Gastrulation begins with the appearance of a latitudinal furrow (usually formed at first of a linear series of small depressions) about 8—10° below the equator of the egg and at first extending through it may be 120° of longitude. The central part of this groove deepens to form the archenteron while its terminal parts flatten out and disappear so that by the time the blastopore is completed (the whole mass of macromeres being now covered in) it forms a short latitudinal opening-crescentic in shape and concave towards the dorsal side owing probably to the more active backgrowth of the central part of the dorsal lip as compared with its two ends.

At a varying period about this time (stages 13—15) a slight flattening in front of the blastopore marks out the position of the medullary plate and by stage 16 definite medullary folds can be seen. For a short period — about stage 18 — varying with different eggs — the folds can be seen to be continuous with one another behind the blastopore or anus (cf. Text-fig. 1).

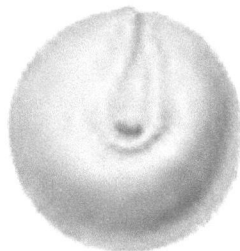

Fig. 1. *Lepidosiren paradoxa*, Stage 16ᵃ. × 8½. View of specimen showing continuity of medullary folds behind blastopore.

In the egg of stage 18 figured the hind end of the embryo has already proceeded too far in its development to show this feature. The head and tail project more prominently in *Protopterus* and in the latter the body of the embryo extends round a considerably greater angular extent of the egg, the tips of the head and tail coming nearly into contact with one another at stage 25 in *Protopterus* while they remain widely separated in *Lepidosiren*.

Conspicuous features in these stages are the cement organ — a crescentic structure on the ventral side — and the external gill rudiments situated on visceral arches III - VI. About stage 23 in *Lepidosiren* a vascular network is seen over the surface of the yolk, its cavities filled with colourless blood there being for some time after its appearance no haemoglobin present.

About the time of hatching (stage 27) the larva has a somewhat tadpole-like shape the hinder tail-like region of the trunk being flexed ventrally. In *Protopterus* a larger proportion of the yolk is concentrated in the anterior swollen part which as a consequence bulges more prominently and the rudiments of various organs — external gills and eyes — are also seen to be relatively larger than in *Lepidosiren*. Within a short space of time after hatching (stage 28) the trunk becomes straightened out and the pinnae of the external gills appear as two rows of little knobs on their external surface. The myotomes are seen to be growing actively in dorsiventral direction.

About stage 30 active growth becomes apparent in the postcoacal or true caudal region which up till this time has been insignificant in size. The limbs make their appearance about stage 31 the pectoral limb being identical in appearance with the external gill rudiments of earlier stages and being at first directly posterior to the external gills as if forming a member of the same series of organs. During the later stages of development the most conspicuous features are the rapid growth of the true tail region, the rapid growth in the head region in front of the main mass of yolk, and the spreading downwards of the myotomes in the lateral wall of the body. With the increase in size of the head region the cement organ becomes carried forwards on its ventral side so as eventually to lie well in front of the opercular opening. The cement organ reaches a great size and forms a very conspicuous feature in the young *Lepidosiren* of stages 32—34. After this atrophy gradually overtakes it and by stage 36 it has completely vanished. The external gills reach their maximum about stages 32—34 in *Protopterus*, rather later (stage 34, 35) in *Lepidosiren*. Thereafter reduction takes place, rapidly in *Lepidosiren*, very slowly in *Protopterus* where vestiges of the three external gills frequently still persist in sexually mature individuals. In *Lepidosiren* there takes place at stage 36 what may be called metamorphosis the external gills undergoing rapid atrophy, the cement organ disappearing, the colouration of the young animal becoming much darker and the habits more lively. Whether there is a similar concentration of developmental change in the case of *Protopterus* is not evident.

The skin. (GRAHAM KERR, 1901 d.)

Up to stage 32—35 in *Lepidosiren* the ectoderm retains its two-layered condition. Thereafter the deep layer cells begin to multiply and the ectoderm gradually assumes the many layered condition of the adult. At about the stage mentioned isolated cells begin to assume a clear glandular character — the forerunners of the great unicellular glands with which the adult epidermis is crowded, and flask glands begin to appear as solid downgrowths of ectoderm which develop a cavity secondarily. Chromatophores which are already present in the mesenchyme show their strongly heliotropic tendencies by wandering towards the surface of the body, crowding together immediately beneath the ectoderm and many of them wandering in between the ectoderm cells from about stage 25 onwards.

A remarkable local development of ectodermal gland cells goes to form the cement organ which is so conspicuous a feature of the young *Protopterus* or *Lepidosiren*. Forming at its first appearance a long crescentic structure spreading across the ventral side of the body, it becomes later on shortened from side to side and is borne in the case of *Lepidosiren* on a conspicuous cushion-like structure. The glandular part of the cement organ arises as a thickening of the deep layer of the ectoderm, the cells of which become tall and columnar, while the superficial layer soon breaks down so as to expose the ends of the gland cells. The atrophy of the organ takes place in the usual way, the glandular epithelium becoming penetrated by vascular loops and invaded by crowds of leucocytes.

Nervous system. (GRAHAM KERR, 1901 d.)

The ectoderm over the whole archenteric region shows as early as stage 13 its deep layer slightly thickened its cells being somewhat columnar forming a wide medullary plate. Later on the axial part of this medullary plate shows active cell multiplication so that a deep solid keel is formed out of which the central nervous system develops. In both *Lepidosiren* and *Protopterus* the definitive cavity of the central nervous system appears as a secondary excavation in the at first solid rudiment. As the front end the rudiment becomes enlarged to form the brain; it soon shows a segmentation into primary forebrain and rhombencephalon. It is not until a much later period that the primitive forebrain shows signs of division into thalamencephalon and mesencephalon. The hemispheres when they appear arise as paired and quite independent bulgings outwards of the wall of the primitive forebrain. During the later stages of development the hemispheres grow rapidly though it is not till much later than the last stage figured that they approach the extraordinary size and complexity (ELLIOT SMITH, 1908) characteristic of the adult. As regards details of brain development it is to be noted that the pineal body is simple. There is no obvious indication of a parapineal body, and there is at no time any trace of eyelike structure. There is a well marked paraphysis closely resembling that of Urodeles and the velum is clearly paired in origin.

Peripheral nerves. (GRAHAM KERR, 1904.)

Lepidosiren with its large cell elements is a very favourable object for studying the development of nerve trunks. Already in stage 24 i. e. while the myotome is still in close contact with the spinal cord the motor trunk can be seen as a naked bridge of soft granular protoplasm continuous at its outer end with the substance of the myotome and at its inner end with that of the spinal cord.

As development goes on this protoplasmic bridge becomes fibrillated — neurofibrils appearing in its substance - it becomes drawn out in length as the myotome recedes from the spinal cord with the growth of the trunk and heavily yolked masses of mesenchymatous protoplasm aggregate round the nerve and spreading along it form the primary sheath.

Olfactory organ. (GRAHAM KERR, 1901 d, 1909.)

The olfactory organ (in *Protopterus*) makes its appearance as seen in external view as a rounded dimple on each side of the under surface of the head some little distance in front of the line of junction of the yolky buccal rudiment with the ectoderm. This dimple becomes gradually elongated to form a groove which passes outwards and backwards.

When the lips begin to grow out the whole of the olfactory grooves become enclosed within the upper lip, the hinder end of the groove soon becoming hidden as the lower jaw grows forwards. The olfactory groove assumes a dumb-bell shape dilated at either end and reduced to a narrow slit in the intervening portion. By the fusion of the edges of the slit-like portion the two dilated ends become separated off as the anterior and posterior nares.

While the openings of the olfactory organ develop in the manner above described it is to be noted that the cavity in the interior of the organ takes its origin as a secondarily arising split in the at first solid rudiment derived from a thickening of the deep layer of the ectoderm. In the later stages of development of the olfactory organ a conspicuous feature is formed by a rounded diverticulum of its lateral wall corresponding closely with the similar structure occurring in the embryo Urodele and possibly homologous with the organ of JACOBSON of amniotic vertebrates.

Eye. (GRAHAM KERR, 1901 d.)

The optic "outgrowth" of the brain is at first solid as is the thalamencephalon at this stage. A cavity develops secondarily in the optic outgrowth and becomes continuous with that which has meanwhile appeared in the thalamencephalon. The lens develops as a solid ingrowth of the deep layer of the ectoderm in which a cavity soon appears secondarily. There is a wide choroid fissure which however closes very soon, and which is restricted to the optic cup. From the size of the individual elements *Lepidosiren* is a very favourable object for studying the development of the visual cells. The main features in the development of the rods have been described and figured in an earlier paper (1901 d).

Otocyst.

The otocyst rudiment becomes apparent about stage 20 as a down growth of the deep layer of the ectoderm. A split is apparent almost from the first and this soon widens out to form a rounded cavity. In the subsequent development of the otocyst the chief point of interest seems to be that the recessus endolymphaticus appears to develop in *Protopterus* and *Lepidosiren* as in *Ceratodus* (SEMON) quite independently of the original connexion of the otocyst with the outer ectoderm. The endolymphatic outgrowth develops considerably mesiad and posterior to the isthmus which forms the last connexion between otocyst and skin.

Skin sense organs.

The system of lateral line organs makes its appearance early in development (*Lepidosiren*, stage 27) as a thickening of the deep layer of the ectoderm on each side anteriorly. This thickening spreads out along the paths marking the adult distribution and becomes divided up into the individual sense organ rudiments. These are at first arranged segmentally in the trunk region. In *Lepidosiren* the organs retain their primitive superficial position while in *Protopterus* they become in the head region eventually sunk beneath the surface in tubular channels.

PINKUS' organ.

AGAR (1906b) has described how the ectodermal outer end of the spiracular cleft becomes converted into the sensory organ of PINKUS.

Pituitary body. (GRAHAM KERR, 1901 d.)

The development of the pituitary body takes place after the normal Amphibian manner. Arising as a wedge shaped ingrowth from the ectoderm about stage 23, the inner end becomes enlarged and develops a cavity as a secondary split. About the same time as the split appears the organ loses its connexion with the skin through its undilated portion undergoing atrophy.

Alimentary canal. (GRAHAM KERR, 1909.)

The differentiation of the alimentary canal out of the primitive mass of yolk may be said to begin about stage 23 with the modelling of its anterior region caused by the precocious development of mesodermal tissues which foreshadows the development of heart and pericardium. In this way the region of the foregut becomes marked off from the midgut which serves as the great storehouse of yolk and which no doubt on this account is much retarded in its differentiation.

Buccal cavity.

The main part of the buccal cavity is developed as a secondary excavation in the originally solid yolkladen anterior part of the enteric rudiment developed from the macromeres. The outer part of the buccal rudiment becomes converted into the epithelial lining of the buccal cavity. Examination of celloidin sections shows that there is no actual ingrowth of ectoderm along the surface of the buccal rudiment. This mode of development of the buccal lining is no doubt secondary but it is of interest as emphasizing the possibility of grave error in using embryological evidence for deciding as to the morphological nature of organs which develop in proximity to the boundary region between two germinal layers. Were the two Dipnoans now under discussion and certain Urodeles the only vertebrates whose embryology had been worked out we might conclude that the vertebrate teeth were originally organs of the endoderm! Apart from their origin the teeth of *Lepidosiren* are of interest in comparison with those of *Ceratodus* in as much as here the primitive condition in which the teeth have not yet fused to form the characteristic dental masses of the adults of existing Dipnoans and which is so beautifully recapitulated in the development of *Ceratodus* is completely slurred over.

The tongue is a "primary tongue" exactly similar to that of the embryos of Urodeles though in this case there is no gland field developed in front of its roots as is the case in the *Amphibia*.

The solid rudiment from which the main part of the buccal cavity is developed by secondary excavation comes in contact with the skin of the ventral surface of the head along a transverse line in front of the outer ends of which the olfactory dimples appear. About stage 34 this area on the ventral side of the head containing the olfactory rudiments becomes enclosed by the lower lip growing forwards while the upper lip appears as a ridge enclosing it in front. By the increased development of these lip rudiments the olfactory openings come to be included in the front part of the definitive buccal cavity.

Visceral clefts.

Six visceral clefts are laid down in the embryo as solid yolk laden rudiments. The fate of the first (Hyomandibular) has been described by AGAR (1906b). It never develops any lumen except at its inner end. It loses its connexion with the skin and, later on, with the pharynx also and eventually its presence is betrayed only by the peculiar PINKUS' organ derived from its outer epiblastic end.

Clefts II—VI become perforated though eventually in *Lepidosiren* II becomes closed, leaving the four clefts which persist in the adult. In *Lepidosiren* the clefts at no time develop regular respiratory lamellae as in most fishes. Their walls grow out into irregular rounded respiratory processes which vary greatly in their extent of development in different individuals.

Lung. (GRAHAM KERR, 1906, 1908, 1909.)

The lung arises as a rounded knob about stage 32 projecting downwards in the middle line from the lower side of the still solid pharynx close to its hind end i. e. on a level with cleft VI. The oesophagus which is already clearly modelled out of the solid mass of yolky endoderm slopes obliquely tailwards, ventralwards and towards the left side. The lung rudiment grows backwards in the median plane, sloping slightly dorsalwards, the oesophagus being bent well out of its way to the left side. Along the dorsal side of the main mass of yolk a way is as it were prepared for the backwardly growing lung by the formation of a kind of valley along which the lung grows. Later on this valley flattens out and disappears. Already soon after its appearance the lung rudiment becomes bilobed and the two lobes grow backwards as the lungs of the adult. Like so many other organs the lung is quite solid at first and only later on develops a cavity in its interior.

Thyroid and thymus.

The thyroid arises from a solid yolk laden rudiment of at first considerable anteroposterior extent which becomes gradually nipped off from the pharynx from behind forwards. The development of the thymus has been described by BRYCE (1905) for *Lepidosiren*. The main thymus buds are derived from the walls of clefts III and IV while abortive buds arise from clefts II and V.

There is a well marked postbranchial body on the left side developed as a solid projection from the pharyngeal rudiment close to the ventral end of cleft VI.

Digestive tract. (GRAHAM KERR, 1909.)

The comparatively undifferentiated stomach arises from the hinder part of the foregut. The yolk-laden region behind this becomes gradually converted by a process of modelling — associated with the ingrowth of mesenchyme into the solid yolk along a spiral line — into the spirally coiled mid-gut. As the differentiation of the mid-gut proceeds the swollen character of its anterior portion containing the main mass of yolk becomes less and less pronounced until at stage 36 the thickest and yolkiest part of the mid-gut is some distance back in the second turn of the spiral. Later (stage 37) the intestine forms in external appearance a straight cylinder the turns of the spirally coiled endodermal tube being now ensheathed in a thick cylindrical wall of connective tissue. By this stage the rectum is slightly dilated and dorsal to it passes forwards the elongated finger shaped rudiment of the cloacal caecum (see p. 10).

Liver.

The liver is in its early stages an outgrowth of the alimentary rudiment anteriorly, becoming distinguishable (about stage 31) by its yolk assuming a fine grained character. An ingrowth of vascular mesoderm cuts off the liver rudiment except for the narrow stalk by which it remains continuous with the gut wall. The liver rudiment rapidly increases in bulk particularly in anteroposterior diameter and it soon loses its at first symmetrical shape and mesial position becoming rotated round so as to lie on the right side of the stomach.

Pancreas.

The dorsal pancreas makes its appearance about stage 32 as a rounded yolk-laden projection from the gut wall dorsally and to the left of the middle line and situated about the level of the posterior nephrostome in *Protopterus*, rather farther back in *Lepidosiren*. In *Lepidosiren* the rudiment, even in early stages, forms a hollow diverticulum of the gut wall while in *Protopterus* it is solid except for a small irregular closed lumen. A little after the appearance of the dorsal pancreas, a pair of ventral rudiments develop, one on each side of the bile duct opening. These latter meet and fuse dorsal to the bile duct and then the dorsal pancreas fuses with the right ventral so as to produce the single pancreatic complex of the adult. By stage 35 the pancreas is penetrated by a network of blood vessels and is becoming histologically differentiated. The most noteworthy feature in the later development of the pancreas is that at no period does it come to project conspicuously beyond the general outline of the gut wall: it remains throughout life concealed within the mesodermal sheath of the gut. This led to its existence being ignored up to the date of PARKER's paper upon the structure of the adult *Protopterus*.

Coelomic organs.

The mesoderm and notochord are represented in early stages (stage 12) by the medium sized blastomeres with medium sized yolk granules which occupy the space between the dorsal wall of the archenteron and the medullary plate, thinning out towards either side and eventually passing laterally without any break into the large blastomeres. This common rudiment of mesoderm and notochord becomes marked off from the endoderm except at its outer edge by a distinct split, while later on (ca. stage 14) another split appears on each side which demarcates the lateral mesoderm rudiment from the median chordal rudiment. Segmentation of the mesoderm on each side begins about stage 17, while the lateral unsegmented mesoderm continues to extend by delamination from the large-yolked cells of the definitive entoderm. The lateral plates meet ventrally under the head about stage 23 but in the trunk region not till much later.

Splanchnocoele.

The splanchnocoele becomes patent first in the pericardiac region, the at first paired pericardiac cavities soon becoming fused. The main part of the splanchnocoele develops by a splitting process of the lateral mesoderm spreading back from the pericardium and downwards from nephrocoeles and myocoeles. In addition to the original communication between pericardium and the main splanchnocoele (pericardio-peritoneal canals) there arises by splitting a secondary more ventral communication. The pericardio-peritoneal canals and the ventral communication become obliterated about stage 34—35, the latter a little later than the former.

Myotomes. (GRAHAM KERR, 1904.)

In the early development of the myotomes there are two features of special interest and importance. There is first the fact that the myoblasts of the inner wall of the myotome are for a time in the form of large neuromyoepithelial cells of the most diagrammatic looking kind — the cell being continued at its inner end into a tail-like process — the motor nerve rudiment. The second feature of interest is that the Dipnoans in question show beyond any possible doubt the development of muscle fibres from the external wall of the myotome. The comparative certainty of observations of this in *Lepidosiren* is due to the fact that the outer ends of the myoblasts of the inner wall of the myotome form a very characteristic broad clear zone which demarcates in the most obvious way the inner wall from the outer wall. A relatively considerable proportion of the substance of the definitive myotome owes its origin to the outer wall.

Details as to the fate of the anterior myotomes, the musculature of the limbs etc. will be found in AGAR (1907). A detail of general morphological interest is the double origin of the constrictor pharyngis (WIEDERSHEIM) a typical "splanchnic" muscle in which as AGAR has shown the dorsal part is actually myotomic in origin.

Nephridial system.

The earliest indications of the kidney system make their appearance about stage 17 in the form of a slight swelling of the mesoderm, producing a faint elevation of the dorsal surface of the embryo on either side. The nephric rudiment so indicated gradually spreads backwards and about stage 22 a well marked difference in size becomes apparent between the swollen headward end of the rudiment which is destined to become the functional pronephros, and the slender hinder portion which forms the pronephric duct. About stage 24 the ducts are seen to have extended right to the cloacal region.

As regards the details of structure in the earliest stages of development of the pronephros I do not feel yet in a position to speak with any confidence owing to the extreme liability of error in investigating the heavily yolk laden tissues. The pronephric rudiment in early stages forms a solid compact mass of mesoderm which as seen in transverse sections forms a somewhat ellipsoidal mass projecting laterally from the nephrotome between the ectoderm and the somatic mesoderm. Appearances point to the nephridial rudiment being formed in the first instance by a series of nephrotomal outgrowths like those described by BRAUER for *Amphibia*, but solid instead of hollow. As many as eight of these segmental tubule rudiments are apparent in some *Lepidosiren* series stretching from myotome II backwards[1]. Except for these early stages which until the technical difficulties in the way of their investigation have been completely overcome

---
1) Traces of at least one tubule may appear in front of this.

must remain somewhat doubtful, the general course of development of the pronephros is fairly clear. About stage 21 the coelomic cavity makes its appearance in the nephrotome and rapidly extends out into the hitherto solid tubule rudiment, and later on back into the archinephric duct. Of the series of nephrotomes which go to compose the pronephric rudiment on each side only two normally proceed with their development to form functional pronephric tubules, the fully developed pronephros being characterized like that of *Ceratodus*, *Polypterus* and many Urodeles by its having two functional tubules. In both *Lepidosiren* and *Protopterus* the pronephric tubules which become functional appear to be those corresponding with myotomes II and IV. As an occasional variation three tubules may be developed (II, III, and IV). In those nephrotomes which develop functional tubules the nephrotome itself goes on developing, its cavity becoming widely patent to form a pronephric chamber. In embryos with three tubules there is seen to be a corresponding series of three pronephric chambers lying one behind the other and at first without any open communication between successive chambers. Later on the pronephric chambers on each side become confluent so that there is now a single chamber stretching through the region occupied by myotomes II, III and IV. The floor of the pronephric chamber becomes pushed upwards about stage 24 by a blood sinus which expands beneath it opposite each nephrostome to form a dome-shaped swelling, the rudiment of the glomerulus. These originally separate glomerular rudiments soon fuse so that each compound pronephric chamber contains a single elongated glomus. By differential growth of the wall of the pronephric chamber the glomus has its point of attachment gradually shifted mediad and dorsad so that by stage 30 it springs from the dorsomedial angle of the chamber i. e. from close to the now median dorsal aorta. As will have been gathered the pronephric chambers or chamber are at first in perfect continuity with the splanchnocoele which spreads outwards from them. Later on as the pronephros becomes greatly enlarged it bulges prominently across the splanchnocoele towards the mesial plane and eventually about stage 32 it comes in contact and fuses with the mesodermal sheath of the alimentary canal. In this way the glomus comes to be enclosed in a secondary pronephric chamber which however remains in free communication with the splanchnocoele at its hinder end. The glomus becomes firmly slung diagonally across this chamber by its tip undergoing fusion with the mesodermal capsule of the pronephros upon the ventrolateral side of the chamber posteriorly.

To return to the pronephros itself. From about stage 26 onwards the pronephros increases rapidly in size owing to the rapid growth in length of the anterior end of the archinephric duct and also — though to a much less extent — of the tubules. The anterior part of the archinephric duct increases so rapidly in length that it becomes greatly convoluted. This marked increase in length of the anterior part of the duct is accompanied by great dilatation of its cavity and thinning of its walls. These phenomena may be correlated with the fact that the cloacal opening becomes closed about the time of hatching and, there being no allantoic or other urinary reservoir posteriorly, the urinary fluid driven out through the still active pronephric tubules has perforce to accumulate in the pronephric duct and causes great distension as it does so. As is well known a similar effect appears to be brought about in some *Amphibia* by an occlusion of the archinephric duct (MARSHALL and BLES). Rapid degeneration of the pronephros now sets in. Its walls assume a waxy appearance, atrophy takes place and by about stage 36 it has practically disappeared although the archinephric duct can still be traced forwards for some distance in front of the mesonephros.

Archinephric ducts.

The question as to how the archinephric duct extends backwards is one to which it is very difficult to find a certain answer. In a perfectly preserved embryo both ectoderm and mesoderm are fitted closely round the archinephric duct. A slight amount of contraction is sufficient to cause the formation of fine chinks between the structures named and it seems a matter of chance whether the duct is left attached to the ectoderm or to the mesoderm or on the other hand is left lying freely between the two layers. No great weight can therefore be given to the fact that the hind end of the duct is attached to one layer or to the other in deciding which layer the duct is originally derived from. There remains the histological character of the duct rudiment and this is clearly mesodermal: the cells forming it being laden with large coarsely granular yolk. This character indicates that the duct is of mesodermal origin. It is in regard to the further question — whether the hind end of the duct grows back freely by its own growth activity — that the chief difficulty arises. The presence of an occasional mitotic figure in the duct rudiment does not necessarily mean that the duct rudiment is doing anything more than merely keeping pace with the general growth of the tissues. If the duct is growing backwards by its own activity all probability points to the growth activity being localised at its hinder end as it is hardly conceivable that the duct can slide bodily backwards between the cells which closely invest it. That there is no such growth activity at the tip of the duct is indicated by the coarsely granular character of the yolk contained in it, because the active metabolism associated with active growth is invariably accompanied by the breaking down of the yolk into a finely granular form so as to be readily assimilable. The probability therefore is that the backgrowth of the duct is effected by delamination from the somatic mesoderm. Junction with the cloaca takes place about stage 24—25 (*Lepidosiren*).

Up till about stage 35 (*Lepidosiren*) the ducts open separately on either side of the cloaca but about this period their cloacal ends are found to be continued backwards into a common portion. About stage 36 (*Lepidosiren*) the region common to the two ducts begins to bulge forwards in front and the projecting part grows actively and forms by stage 37 a long tubular cloacal caecum. With further growth of the animal the caecum becomes wider and gradually assumes the rounded form characteristic of the adult.

Mesonephros.

The mesonephric tubules arise as at first solid rudiments, arranged roughly segmentally and not showing at any period continuity with the myotomes. In *Protopterus* they begin about segment 14 but in occasional specimens nuclear condensations have been seen in segments anterior to this (as far forward as the hinder limit of the pronephros) which may possibly represent vestigial tubules. The definitive tubule rudiments become obvious about stage 30. They are at first quite solid and are independent of the duct. Each rudiment assumes a C-shape, a split develops in its interior and its outer end undergoes fusion with the wall of the archinephric duct, the cavity of the tubule and that of the duct soon (stage 31 *Lepidosiren*) becoming continuous. The free end of the tubule now becomes dilated to form the Malpighian body (stage 32 *Lepidosiren*) and after a time (stage 35 *Lepidosiren*) the glomerulus is formed by a pushing in of the wall of the Malpighian cavity.

Genital ducts.

The development of the genitorenal connections of the male and of the oviduct in the female has not yet been worked out. In stage 37 (*Lepidosiren*) the oviducal funnel is present. It passes back into a solid Müllerian duct rudiment which at its hind end appears to die away amongst the mesenchyme.

Gonads.

The development of the gonads has not yet been worked out. In stage 38 (*Lepidosiren*) a cylindrical strand of gonad with large spherical nuclei rich in chromatin is clearly visible ventral to the mesonephros.

Organs of the mesenchyme.

As investigation of these organs is not yet nearly complete I shall content myself with referring only very briefly to some of the more important skeletal features which have been determined.

Skeleton.

It will be recalled that the notochord arises from the axial portion of the mass of medium sized blastomeres lying dorsal to the archenteron. By stage 14 in *Lepidosiren* the mesoderm has become marked off on each side by a split, the notochordal rudiment now forming a ridge like projection of the archenteric roof. About stage 16 the chorda becomes split off from the thin layer of endoderm beneath it which persists as the enteric roof. By about stage 23 the notochord has become cylindrical and a delicate primary sheath is formed on its surface. As AGAR (1906 a) has shown, the front end of the notochord degenerates leaving the sheath anteriorly filled with mesenchyme. Later on as the chordal cells increase in size as they become vacuolated the notochord pushes its way forward again into the sheath, occupying the position of the original front end which had degenerated and disappeared. About stage 32 the secondary sheath makes its appearance. It rapidly increases in thickness and about stage 36 (*Lepidosiren*) begins to be colonized by immigrant amoeboid cartilage cells from the arcualia, becoming eventually converted into a continuous cylinder of cartilage. It is to be noted that the intracranial part of the secondary notochordal sheath becomes colonized by cartilage cells from the parachordals in precisely similar fashion. In the head region the trabeculae appear first. The quadrate region of the mandibular arch is from the first continuous with the trabeculae. A faint rudiment of the palatopterygoid outgrowth appears but soon disappears again (AGAR). The suspension of the jaw apparatus is entirely by means of the upper end of the mandibular arch (protostylic, GRAHAM KERR, 1907 b [1]); or autostylic — GREGORY, 1904 — condition). The chondrocranium shows progressive development towards the adult condition without signs of retrogression.

Bone first makes its appearance about stage 32—34 in *Lepidosiren* in the form of thin sheaths investing the base of the skull (parasphenoid) the pectoral girdle and hyoid arch, on the inner face of the lower jaw (splenial) and along the side of the head from the quadrate forwards ("palatopterygoid" bone). By stage 37 all of the individual bones of the adult skull have developed.

---

[1] I was unaware at the time of GREGORY's paper of 1904, which renders my note in great part unnecessary.

Tables.

Lepidosiren

Stage	External features	Segmentation cavity	Invagination	Archenteron	Dorsal wall of archenteron	External form
2	First meridional furrow.					
3	Second meridional furrow.					
4	First four vertical furrows.					
7	Egg completely segmented.	Hardly any chinks between blastomeres.				
9	Late segmentation.	Appears as a larger chink amongst the blastomeres.				
11		Fully developed. Becomes traversed by spongework of macromeres about stage 12.)	Continuous latitudinal groove which may reach 120° in length.			
13		Practically obliterated. Reduced to a few chinks.	Blastopore reduced in length; crescentic slit concave dorsally.	135° in length. (In other specimens of same external appearance 103°, 105°, 100°, 120°, 140°.) Inner end rounded with continuous cuticle.	Composed of large-yolked cells. Roof cells large yolked, agreeing in character with rest of endoderm, not with ectoderm.	
14			Much shorter. Large yolk cells almost completely hidden.		(Mesoderm split off from endoderm except at outer edge; also separated by a split from the notochordal rudiment.)	
16			Beginning to be enclosed by medullary folds.		(Mesoderm and notochord distinct.)	
18	Branchial eminence appears. (Pronephric swelling appears 17.)		Reduced to short slit-like opening.	225°.		
20						Medullary folds have completely met.

paradoxa.

Metotic mesoderm segments	Nervous system	Eye	Otocyst	Visceral clefts	Urogenital system	Stage
						2
						3
						4
						7
						9
						11
	Deep layer of ectoderm of medullary plate decidedly thickened and beginning to be more than one cell thick.					13
	(Very slight longitudinal depression along centre of medullary plate. The latter has grown down into a distinct keel by multiplication of its deep layer cells in the region of the mesial plane.)					14
Mesoderm not yet segmented.	Medullary folds distinct. Medullary keel well developed.					16
Mesoderm segments (about 7) faintly discernible with central coelomic cavity beginning to appear.	Medullary folds have met along middle of trunk region.					18
About 12? Myocoeles present widely open.	Neural rudiment still solid.	Solid optic rudiment.	Begins as downgrowth of deep layer of ectoderm.	(3 solid rudiments [AGAR].)	Pronephric swelling opposite anterior segments.	20

Stage	External features	Cement organ	Meiotic segments	Nervous system	Eye	Otocyst	Nose
21	Optic rudiments visible.			Still solid.	(Rudiment with indications of a split in its interior.)	(Rudiment apparent with indications of split.)	
23	Head and tail folds becoming distinct. Branchial eminence becoming segmented.	Cement organ rudiment as slight thickening of deep layer of ectoderm.	About 24. (Sclerotome appears.)	Central canal now extensive, dilated in rhombencephalon and extending through about ⅔ of the length of the neural rudiment. (24. Motor nerve trunks apparent as protoplasmic bridges.)	Split dilated to form definite cavity.	(Split dilated to form definite cavity.)	
25	Tail fold becoming more prominent than head. External gill rudiments appear as knob-like projections from visceral arches III – VI.	Cement organ clearly visible in a external view crescentic with longitudinal groove. Superficial ectoderm breaking down.	About 47. Inner wall of myotome of flattened cells stretching throughout myotome. (Sclerotome spreading up internal to myotome.)	Transverse fold of brain floor appears in front of rhombencephalon. (Nerve fibres appear in spinal cord and motor trunks.) (26. Hemisphere rudiments as slight bulgings outwards of side walls of thalamencephalon.)	Retina becoming thickened. (Lens thickening begins to appear in ectoderm.)	Widely expanded thin-walled sac still connected by stalk with ectoderm.	Paired thick downgrowth of deep layer of ectoderm with radiating arrangement of columnar cells; their inner ends clear of yolk. Cavity represented by traces of split.
27 Hatching.	Hatching. (First spontaneous movements about two days previous.)		About 55. Contractile fibres in inner walls of myotome.	(Sheath mesenchyme begins to collect near motor trunks. Hemispheres present as lateral bulgings of wall of primary forebrain.)		(Otocyst still connected with ectoderm. Ductus endolymphaticus beginning to sprout out.)	
28 Three day larva.	Hind part of trunk straightened out and growing rapidly.		About 59.		Lens rudiment as distinct thickening of deep layer of ectoderm. Retina much thickened.	Otocyst still connected with ectoderm. Ductus endolymphaticus as slight projection quite separate from connection with ectoderm.	Cavity as a slight split, closed. Superficial layer of ectoderm continuous over rudiment.

Normal Plates of the Development of Lepidosiren paradoxa and Protopterus annectens. 15

Hypophysis	Enteron	Notochord	Visceral clefts	Splanchnocoele	Urogenital system	Heart and Vessels	Stage
							21
	Foregut becoming folded off from rest of endoderm by a small space developing beneath its anterior end.	(Separated from rest endoderm, circular in transverse section, cells flat and plate-like. Primary sheath has appeared.)			(Pronephric tubules developing; pronephric chambers not continuous; duct does not reach cloaca.)		23
(Ingrowth just commencing.)	Foregut well folded off from rest of endoderm.		(Six solid cleft rudiments. Last two not yet completely fused with ectoderm.)	Spacious pericardiac cavity, two halves fused except behind.	Pronephros with two funnels. Pronephric chambers continuous (Glomerulus still in two segmental pieces.) Archinephric ducts are open into cloaca.	Heart rudiment with a few corpuscles free in lumen. Vessels of external gills also apparent and with a few corpuscles.	25
	Anus closed.		Six solid cleft rudiments.		(Gleenus no longer segmented.) Archinephric duct tortuous towards its front end.	Dorsal aorta, as solid heavily yolked rudiment.)	27
	Anus closed.		Cleft rudiments solid.		Archinephric duct coiled in region of pronephros.	Dorsal aorta with lumen and scattered corpuscles.	28

Stage	Length	External features	Chondral skeleton	Bony skeleton	Nervous system	Integument	Eye	Otocyst	Nose	Hypophysis	Mouth
30 Ten day larva.	19 mm	Growth of postanal region commencing. External gills becoming raised up on a common base. Mouth indicated by groove.			Hemispheres growing forward but not yet reaching anterior limit of forebrain. Posterior root ganglia developed.	Rudiments of epidermal sense organs present. (Dermis beginning to appear.)	Lens still solid thickening of deep layer of ectoderm. Slight traces of pigment appearing in posterior wall of optic cup.	Endolymphatic outgrowth has appeared medio-dorsally. Otocyst has lost its connexion with ectoderm.	Narrow cavity has developed	With distinct lumen. Curves round tip of infundibulum.	Outer cells of solid buccal rudiment begin to take on an ectoderm-like character.
31 Thirteen day larva. (12–15 days.)	20 mm	Median fin fold much increased in size. Appearance of limbs and of opercular fold. Scattered chromatophores on dorsal side of head and anterior trunk region.			Pineal rudiment and paraphysis developed. Hemispheres project beyond the limit of the primary forebrain.		Pigment present in hind wall of optic cup. Lens detached from ectoderm. Hind wall thickened.		Cavity well marked definite closed. Dimple visible on external surface.		Solid. Faint indications of tooth germs.
32 Twenty four day larva.	24 mm	Operculum growing backwards. Cement organ prominent. Actively functional. Chromatophores scattered over whole dorsal surface.	Trabeculae. Mandibular and hyoid arches.	Parasphenoid.		Chromatophores in ectoderm.	Rods not yet developed.		Slit-like aperture along ventral side of olfactory organ.		Lumina in buccal rudiments but not continuous. Tooth germs well developed. (Appearance of enamel cap.)

Normal Plates of the Development of Lepidosiren paradoxa and Protopterus annectens.

Digestive tract and liver	Pancreas	Visceral clefts	Thyroid	Post-branchial bodies	Lung	Urogenital system	Heart and vessels	Myotomes	Splanchno-coele	Stage
Gut rudiment solid except in neighbourhood of openings of archinephric ducts. Anus closed. Liver rudiment split off from main mass of yolk. Postanal gut becoming reduced.		Solid.	In form of solid projection of pharyngeal floor.			Attachment of pronephric glomerulus now medio-dorsal. (Mesonephric tubule rudiments make their appearance.)	Heart a simple curved tube; contractile fibrils in myocardium. Dorsal aorta dilated but not yet quite circular in section. (29+. Six aortic arches developed.)	(Eye muscles indicated by condensations of mesenchyme. AGAR.)	(Lateral plates not yet met in trunk: split in anterior segments. Cavity continued as pericardio-peritoneal ducts into pericardium. AGAR.)	30
Liver distinguished from main yolk by fine grained yolk. Traversed by rich network of blood vessels. (Gut lumen only in cloacal region.) Postanal gut disappeared.		Solid.	Solid, still connected by narrow neck with buccal rudiment in front of root of tongue.	(Yolky rudiment on left side projecting forwards from side of pharyngeal floor ventrally; left point projecting farther back than right.	Rudiment solid in front; with split like cavity behind; bicuspid posteriorly; left point projecting farther back than right.	Lumen appearing as split in some mesonephric tubule rudiments. Most still solid. Some becoming fused with archinephric duct at outer end. Anterior end of archinephric duct and pronephric tubules much distended. (31+, AGAR. Pronephrocoeles open to pericardium by pericardio-peritoneal ducts; about 26 tubule rudiments.)	Blood red. (Mandibular and hyoidean aortic arches reduced.) (31+. Posterior cardinals beginning to fuse.)	Outer wall beginning to thicken and to develop contractile fibrils. Inner wall myoblasts converted almost entirely into fibrils. Mesenchyme beginning to wander in between myotomes.	(31 + Pronephric chamber open to pericardium by pericardio-peritoneal ducts. Ventral communication between pericardium and main splanchnocoele in addition to pericardio-peritoneal ducts. AGAR.)	31
Buccal lumen developed but not yet open to exterior. Extends back into pharynx but not to glottis. In midgut lumen between pylorus and liver, then solid nearly to cloacal region. Small lumen rounded in section and varying in thickness developed for short distance in front of cloaca. Spiral groove developed slightly at hind end. Shallow dorsal valley along midgut in which the lungs lie.	Yolky projection from dorsal side of gut rudiment of midline and just behind opening of foregut into midgut. Wide cavity which opens into gut lumen.	No clefts perforate. Cleft II almost perforate.			Yolky rudiment on left side. Isolated from pharynx. Blood vessels beginning to penetrate.	Lung rudiment well developed with wide lumen reaching to glottis double except at its front end.	Two pronephrostomes; archinephric duct much dilated in front. (Secondary pronephric chamber open behind into splanchnocoele.) Some mesonephric tubules have developed a lumen, open into archinephric duct at one end and are slightly dilated at the other to form the rudiment of the Malpighian body.	Heart still tubular. (Rich vitelline network covering ventral and lateral aspects of gut. Drains anteriorly into large irregular subintestinal vein which passes into liver. Right anterior cardinal in front much larger than left.)			32

Stage	Length	External features	Chondral skeleton	Bony skeleton	Nervous system	Integument	Eye	Otocyst	Nose	Hypophysis	Pineal body	Mouth
34 Twenty seven day larva.	30 mm.	Darkly coloured except ventral side of trunk which is still without pigment. Cement organ about maximum.	Floor and side walls of cranium cartilaginous. Lower jaw, hyoid, occipital, arch and rib also cartilaginous. Skeleton of fore-limb marked out by condensation of nuclei.	"Palatopterygoid" extending back to quadrate. Splenial present on inner side of MECKEL's cartilage. Pectoral girdle commencing to be ensheathed in bone.	Paraphysis becoming reduced. Sheath of motor trunks much attenuated.	Ectoderm still mostly two-layered except in head region.	Lens nearly fills cup; small amount of mesenchyme.	Ductus endolymphaticus with swollen end in contact with hindbrain roof laterally. Semicircular canals formed. Thickened maculae in floor.	Lips of nasal opening have fused except at ends so as to separate anterior and posterior nares. External diverticulum present.			Open.
35 Thirty day larva.	ca. 36 mm.	External gills at maximum development. Cement organ much reduced. Pelvic limbs much increased in length.	(Arcualia present.) Chorda cells becoming vacuolar.	Hyoid ensheathed in bone.	Commencing ingrowth of lateral plexus into ventricle.	(Commencing development of unicellular glands.)		Rods developing.				
36 Forty day larva.	ca. 41 mm.	Metamorphosis. Pigment advances to ventral side. Atrophy of external gills. Pigment much denser.	Olfactory capsule cartilaginous. Secondary sheath of notochord becoming colonized by immigrant cells from arcualia. Neural spines developed, continuous anteriorly with arcualia.	Fronto-parietalia not yet developed.				Ductus endolymphaticus with end divided into lobes.				

Normal Plates of the Development of Lepidosiren paradoxa and Protopterus annectens.

Teeth	Digestive tract and liver	Pancreas	Visceral clefts	Thyroid	Post-branchial bodies	Thymus	Lung	Urogenital system	Heart and vessels	Myotomes	Splanchnocoele	Stage
Teeth calcified. Bony trabeculae at their bases.	Oesophagus solid behind glottis. Pharynx with lumen in middle (but solid laterally) reaching back to widely open glottis. Lumen rounded in region of stomach — extending into midgut for short distance. Solid back to near cloacal region.	Ventral rudiments present.	II widely open. III closed still by thin membrane. IV, V, VI solid.	Interpenetrated by intrusive connective tissue with blood vessels.	Isolated.	Thymus bud of cleft III developed.	Glottis open.	Three pronephrostomes on right; two on left. (Normally two on each side.)		Outer wall thick, many layers of muscle cylinders.	Ventral communication between pericardiac coelom and main splanchnocoele.	34
Well developed but still covered by buccal epithelium.	Pharynx with wide lumen though still snugfit at edge. Oesophagus with small discontinuous lamina. In stomach large continuous lumen opening into wide irregular lumen of midgut which stretches back for some distance but not yet continuous with cloacal cavity. Intestine deeply incised by spiral ingrowth of mesenchyme. Liver greatly increased in size extending back dorsal to gut on right side. Gall bladder showing on surface ventrally.	Pancreas much lobed and tubular in places. In some parts the cells have assumed the definitive character of pancreas cells and are functional.	Clefts II, III, IV, V, VI open, VI by very narrow chink.	Highly vascular follicles, well developed.	Nearly free from yolk. Penetrated by blood vessels.	Thymus bud increased in size. (Rudiment on cleft II. BRYCE.)	Functional. Extends back about ⅔ distance from glottis to cloaca. Walls thin and membranous and widely dilated except close to hind end where growing actively.	Pronephrostomes still open, Mesonephric tubules much elongated forming compact gland. Glomeruli fully developed. Archinephric ducts opening into cloaca independently on each side.	Ventricular spongework present.		Pericardiac coelom shut off from main splanchnocoele.	35
Projecting into buccal cavity but covered by epithelial sheath.	Liver and stomach have been rotated so that liver lies now to the right of the stomach which is consequently visible from the ventral side. Liver growing rapidly backwards. Oesophageal lumen still discontinuous.		Clefts II—VI open. (In other specimens of this stage II is becoming closed.)		Yolk gone. Penetrated by blood vessels.	Main thymus bud divided into of lobes. Bud also present from cleft IV.	Reaches back as far as hinder end of spiral part of gut.	Pronephros very degenerate and shrunken. Pronephric chambers reduced to small anteriorly projecting diverticula of splanchnocoele, on the walls of which traces of the degenerate nephrostomes are still visible. Archinephric ducts unite posteriorly and common portion is dilated bulging slightly forwards as rudiment of cloacal caecum.				36

Protopterus

Stage	External features	Segmentation cavity	Invagination	Archenteron	Dorsal wall of archenteron	Cement organ	Metotic mesoderm segments	Nervous system
VII	Completely segmented.	Chinks between blastomeres.						
IX	Advanced segmentation.	Large segmentation cavity with thin 2-layered roof.						
XI		At its maximum.	Long longitudinal groove.	Shallow slit just beginning to bend dorsalwards at its inner end.				
XIII		Almost obliterated reduced to chinks between blastomeres.	Slightly concave towards dorsal side. Patch of macromeres still exposed.	Rounded at its inner end. 165° (in other specimens of same stage down to 65°).				
XIV			Short crescentic blastopore. Macromeres completely covered in.	135°				(Deep layer of ectoderm columnar in medullary plate region.)
XVI			Blastopore a short latitudinal slit.	255°	Mesoderm rudiment on each side marked off by its more rounded cells from the more compact enteric roof and notochordal rudiment.			Medullary folds make their appearance. Medullary keel well developed.
XVIII	Faint swellings in position of external gills and pronephros.			290°	Notochord not yet split off from endoderm.		About seven.	Thick solid rudiment of brain and spinal cord. Medullary folds have met except posteriorly where they diverge to surround blastopore.
XX	Medullary folds fused. Pronephric swelling more elongated.						About 10. Anterior 2 with widely open myocoeles.	Solid.
XXI	Optic outgrowths indicated by slight bulging of surface. Head region projecting more distinctly above general surface.						About 17. Myocoeles developed anteriorly.	
XXIII	Branchial eminence becoming segmented. Tip of head projecting markedly: tail end beginning to project. T-shaped pronephros with duct slightly curved. Duct does not yet reach hind end?					Rudiment present as slight tickening of deep layer of ectoderm.	24. Inner wall cells flattened, plate-like.	Lumen definite in spinal cord and narrow split forming in brain.

annectens.

Eye	Otocyst	Enteron	Notochord	Visceral cleft	Splanchnocoele	Urogenital system	Stage
							VII
							IX
							XI
							XIII
							XIV
							XVI
							XVIII
(Slight solid projection.)	Downgrowth of deep layer of ectoderm.						XX
Optic rudiment solid.		Stretches through 305°.	Notochord cells becoming flattened. Faint indication of primary sheath. Chorda still continuous with endoderm anteriorly.				XXI
Optic rudiment with narrow lumen. Inner wall very slightly thickened.	Otocyst with definite rounded cavity surrounded by thick wall.	Foregut beginning to be marked off by development of a small space ventral to it.	Chorda cells flattened platelike.	Three solid rudiments of clefts I–III; common rudiment of IV, V and VI.	Paired pericardiac cavities present.	Solid pronephric rudiment with two tubules. Nephrocoele beginning to form opposite first tubule.	XXIII

Normentafeln zur Entwicklungsgeschichte der Wirbeltiere.

Stage	Length	External features	Cement organ	Metotic segments	Chondral skeleton	Nervous system	Integument	Eye	Otocyst	Nose
XXV		Head and tail folds projecting markedly so as nearly to meet. Anus hidden by tail fold. Cement organ visible as long crescentic structure.	Present as thickening of deep layer of ectoderm; superficial layer gone from surface over gland.	About 29. Myocoeles patent. Myoblasts flat yolky cells stretching whole length of myotome.		Cavity of central nervous system developed. Primary fore brain marked off.		Anterior (retinal) wall of rudiment slightly thickened.	Otocyst with wide definite cavity.	Slight thickening of deep layer of ectoderm.
XXVII Hatching.		Larva tadpole-shaped with hind part of trunk flexed ventrally. External gills projecting markedly. Dorsal ridge of body containing myotomes much more prominent.		38.		Brain slightly more advanced than fig. B (stage 28)in Lepidosiren GRAHAM KERR, 1901 d.		Retina much thickened not involuted. (Lens not yet apparent.)	Still continuous with ectoderm by narrow isthmus. (In other specimens of this stage the ductus endolymphaticus is visible as a small outgrowth from otocyst dorsally.)	Solid ingrowth of deep layer of ectoderm.
XXVIII During first day of larval life.		Hind end of body nearly straight. Pinnae of external gill appearing as double series of small knobs on their external side.						Lens rudiment as yolky thickening of deep layer of ectoderm. Retina cells long columnar, free from yolk at their ends towards lens.	Otocyst still in contact with ectoderm.	Olfactory rudiment as much thickened deep layer of ectoderm; distal ends of columnar cells becoming free from yolk. Superficial layer of ectoderm still continuous over rudiment.
XXIX About end of first day larval life.	A little over 9 mm.	Median fin fold more developed. No appreciable increase of post-anal region.				Hemispheres not yet reaching level of anterior limit of primary fore brain.	Ectoderm two-layered.	Lens yolky thickening of deep layer of ectoderm. Inner ends of retinal cells beginning to be freed from yolk.	Otocyst still in contact with ectoderm. Ductus endolymphaticus as wide outgrowth from mediodorsal wall much posterior to point where in contact with ectoderm.	Thickening of deep layer of ectoderm. Distal ends of cells becoming free from yolk. Superficial layer of ectoderm still continuous over olfactory rudiments.
XXXI Two day larva.	11 mm.	Pinnae of external gills elongated. Postanal region increasing in length.			Notochord with thin primary sheath.	Hemispheres have nearly reached level of anterior limit of primary fore brain. Paraphysis present. Hind brain roof thin and membranous.	Ectoderm two-layered.	Lens with rounded lumen. Intrusive mesenchyme in optic cup.	Isolated from skin.	Open to exterior. Superficial ectoderm broken down over opening.

Normal Plates of the Development of Lepidosiren paradoxa and Protopterus annectens.

Hypophysis	Enteron	Notochord	Mouth	Digestive tract and Liver	Visceral cleft	Lung	Urogenital system	Heart and Vessels	Myotomes	Splanchnocoele	Stage
	Foregut longer owing to extension back beneath it of pericardium.	Notochord of flat yolky cells. Primary sheath distinct.			Cleft rudiments present but not easily distinguishable from intervening mesenchyme.		Two tubules and duct with distinct lumen.	First trace of heart visible as involuted thickening of ventral walls of pericardium containing rudiment of endocardium.		Pericardiac cavities fused.	XXV
Simple wedge-shaped.	Anus open. Pharynx solid. Lumen from this back. Dilated behind pericardium.				Six solid rudiments.		Two pronephric tubules. (In one case 3 tubules opposite segments 2, 3 and 4. Duct showing beginning of coiling anteriorly. Lumen extends to cloaca.)	Main vessels laid down also network of vessels developed in parts on surface with distinct flattened endothelium. Large masses of spherical cells on surface of yolk-young corpuscles spherical and full of yolk. Dorsal aorta dilated in places but cavity not continuous.			XXVII
Becoming constricted off.	Pharynx solid. Small lumen back from this. Anus open.				Cleft rudiments solid.		(Anterior end of archinephric duct elongating and becoming coiled. Two tubules forming T-piece.)	Dorsal aorta dilated with fluid but very few corpuscles in it.			XXVIII
At tip of infundibulum: solid.				Gut solid except between cloacal opening and opening of archinephric ducts. Post-anal gut large solid.	Still solid.		Anterior end of duct becoming coiled. Glomus attached to floor of pronephric chamber towards its mesial side.	Dorsal aorta with wide lumen circular in section. Heart S-shaped tube bifurcating at each end.	Contractile fibrils along dorsal and ventral surfaces of myoblasts.	Cavity of pericardium extends back for some distance on each side (pericardio-peritoneal ducts). Lateral plate unsplit in trunk.	XXIX
		Buccal rudiment still solid.		Alimentary canal solid except in cloacal region, with traces of cavity here and there elsewhere.	Cleft rudiment still solid.	Not yet apparent.	Two nephrostomes. Rudiments of mesonephric tubules.	Corpuscles laden with yolk.	Contractile fibrils have appeared in myoblasts.	Pronephric chamber continuous with pericardium by pericardio-peritoneal ducts.	XXXI

Stage	Length	External features	Chondral skeleton	Bony skeleton	Nervous system	Integument	Eye	Otocyst	Nose	Hypophysis	Pineal body	Mouth
XXXIII 6 day larva.	14 mm.	Cloacal opening lateral. Postanal region much elongated. Median fin fold ditto. First rudiments of limbs visible in external view.	Limb axis marked out by nuclear condensation.		Hemispheres project forwards beyond level of anterior end of primary fore brain. Pineal organ developed.	(Chromatophores present on dorsal side of head.)	Hind wall of lens vesicle much thickened. Pigment present in pigment layer of retina. Mesenchyme in optic cup highly vascular.	Canals beginning to bulge. Macular thickenings appearing.	Slit-like opening.			Solid. Tooth germs apparent.
XXXIV 7 day larva.	16 mm.	Front part of trunk shrinking relatively. Limbs now project freely. Opercular fold distinct.	Mandibular and hyoid arch, pectoral girdle, base of skull, auditory capsule.				(Rods developing in centre of retina.)					Lumen developed back into pharynx but not freely open to exterior although slight slit present. Lip fold projects down on each side enclosing external naris. Lower jaw beginning to grow forwards.
XXXV 9 day larva.	19 mm.	Anterior part of trunk now only slightly bulging. Pectoral limb extends back beyond external gills.		Bony trabeculae at tooth bases spreading along jaws and in region of parasphenoid.	Commencing ingrowth of lateral plexus into ventricles of hemispheres.	Chromatophores.	Rods developed.	Endolymphatic ducts pass dorsalwards towards midline over hind brain roof. Outgrowths foreshadowed by slight bulgings? Canals formed.	External diverticulum present.	Wide lumen.		Freely open.
XXXVI	22 mm.	Bulging of anterior part of trunk region has disappeared. Cement organ has disappeared. Limbs and tail long and slender. Median fin fold very prominent.	Occipital arch in contact dorsally with auditory capsule. Branchial arches 1—4 present. Neural spines continuous with arches. Secondary sheath of notochord not yet invaded by cartilage cells.	Thin parasphenoid in maxilla. Palatopterygoid. Bone ensheathing hyoid occipital rib and on inner side of MECKEL's cartilage. Also on ventral face of lower end of pectoral girdle.				Endolymphatic ducts reach dorsal midline and short outgrowths are developed on them.		(Isolated; lying posterodorsal to hyoid arch.)		

Teeth	Digestive tract and liver	Pancreas	Visceral clefts	Thyroid	Post-branchial bodies	Thymus	Lung	Urogenital system	Heart and vessels	Myotomes	Splanchnocoele	Stage
	Endoderm solid except in region of cloaca. Liver rudiment growing forwards beneath pericardium.	Round yolky projection containing small lumen in its centre. Attached to gut dorsally by narrow stalk at level of hinder pronephrostome to left of mesial plane and projecting towards right.	All solid.	Solid yolky rudiment.	Heavily yolked solid rudiment arising from floor of pharynx, stretching from root of cleft VI forwards to cleft V on left side.		Rounded projection from mid ventral surface of pharynx stretches back alongside oesophageal rudiment; small closed cavity formed by cytolysis in centre. No bilobing.	Mesonephric rudiments.	Vitelline network of vessels over surface of yolk. (Right posterior cardinal larger than left in front. Right and left connected by cross channels.)			XXXIII
Teeth germs with calcareous matter.	Liver rudiment with fine yolk.	Dorsal pancreatic rudiment with thick yolky wall and large definite cavity. Ventral rudiments solid.	Solid.	(Connection with pharynx reduced to slender cord or broken through.)	Still solid, yolky, connected with pharynx by a narrow neck. Projects forwards and downwards from its attachment, in contact with hind wall of aortic arch VI.		Wide lumen but no glottis; pharynx being solid at this level. (Lung rudiment distinctly bilobed, extending back short distance behind posterior nephrostome.)	(Archinephric ducts much coiled anteriorly. About 12 mesonephric rudiments.)	(Right posterior cardinal larger and anastomosing with left.)		Pericardiac coelom isolated from main splanchnocoele and from pronephric chamber.	XXXIV
Bodies of teeth well developed.	Pharyngeal lumen not yet continuous in front of glottis. Behind glottis for some distance nearly solid. Liver with rich vascular network. Wide bile duct.	Pancreas compact penetrated by vascular network, undergoing histological differentiation. Three rudiments fused together.	Cleft I solid except for PINKUS' organ. Removed from skin. Still in connection with pharynx. II and III open, IV nearly perforate; V and VI solid.	Isolated, vascular.	No longer yolky. Penetrated by blood vessels.	Buds present at dorsal ends of clefts II and (larger) III.	Glottis open. Lungs with thin vascular walls extending back nearly half the distance from glottis to cloaca.	Pronephric chamber posterior to main mass of pronephric coils. Much connective tissue between coils: also in glomerulus. Nephrostomes still open with flagella, though walls degenerating. Anterior nephrostome opens into pronephric chamber at extreme front end. Posterior back near hind end of glomerulus. (Archinephric ducts unite close to opening into cloaca.)		Myotomes have not yet met ventrally in trunk.	Pericardiac coelom isolated from main splanchnocoele and from pronephric chamber.	XXXV
Teeth project into buccal cavity but are covered by epithelial sheath.		Pancreas much larger lying in dorsal groove of gut. Forms mass of branched secretory tubes with fine lumen, separated by conspicuous connective tissue containing blood vessels.	II–V perforate (IV barely perforate). III very wide. PINKUS' organ isolated from pharynx.	Thyroid isolated, secreting.	Open sponge work with blood vessels in meshes.		Bud from cleft II small. That of III much enlarged.	Extend back rather more than half way to cloaca.				XXXVI

Conclusion.

In comparing together the Normentafeln of the three Dipnoi it will be seen at once how the close affinity between *Lepidosiren* and *Protopterus* is brought out clearly in their developmental features. Their whole course of development — segmentation, gastrulation, the modelling of the body of the embryo, the characters of the larvae with their external gills and cement organ, and the internal details of development so far as known — alike attest the naturalness of the group *Dipneumona*.

Just as striking are the differences which mark off the developmental phenomena of *Lepidosiren* and *Protopterus* from those of *Ceratodus*. In the latter the segmentation departs less from the equal holoblastic type, the external features of gastrulation approach more near to those of the typical amphibian, and striking differences are to be seen in the early larval stages. There is an absence of the tadpole shaped stage so characteristic of *Lepidosiren* and *Protopterus* due to the fact that the yolk is in *Ceratodus* distributed more equally along the length of the midgut rudiment. And with the absence of concentration of the yolk towards the headward end of the midgut it is seen that the whole head region in *Ceratodus* proceeds more rapidly in its development, while in *Protopterus* and *Lepidosiren* it is caused to lag behind in comparison.

Apart from such general differences, the numerous differences in details of structure are enough to make it plain that a deep cleft separates the monopneumona from the dipneumona although in my opinion there still exists ample reason for retaining them as subdivisions of a single group.

List of Papers dealing with the Morphology of the Dipnoi published during the years 1900—1909.

For the sake of convenience I have endeavoured to include in the following list all papers (excluding mere Referats) dealing with the Ontogeny of the Dipnoi even though included in SEMON's Bibliography. In compiling the list I have had the valuable assistance of Dr. R. H. TRAQUAIR F. R. S. who has most kindly furnished the necessary palaeontological references and to whom I have much pleasure in offering my acknowledgments and grateful thanks.

1906a AGAR, W. E., The development of the Skull and Visceral arches in *Lepidosiren* and *Protopterus*. Trans. R. Soc. Edinb., XLV, p. 49—64.

1906b AGAR, W. E., The spiracular gill cleft in *Lepidosiren* and *Protopterus*. Anat. Anzeiger, XXVIII, p. 298—304.

1907 AGAR, W. E., The development of the anterior mesoderm and paired fins with their nerves in *Lepidosiren* and *Protopterus*. Trans. R. Soc. Edinb., XLV, p. 611—639.

1908 AGAR, W. E., On the appearance of Vascular Filaments on the Pectoral Fin of *Lepidosiren paradoxa*. Anat. Anzeiger, XXXIII, p. 27—30.

1904 BING, R., and BURCKHARDT, R., Das Zentralnervensystem von *Ceratodus forsteri*. Anat. Anzeiger, XXV, p. 588—599.

1905 BING, R., and BURCKHARDT, R., Das Zentralnervensystem von *Ceratodus forsteri*. SEMON's Zoologische Forschungsreisen, I, p. 509—600.

1903 BLUNTSCHLI, H., Eisenhämatoxylin- und Bronde-Präparate der Leber von *Ceratodus forsteri* und *Acipenser ruthenus*. Verh. anat. Ges., XVII, p. 198, 199.

1904 BLUNTSCHLI, H., Der feinere Bau der Leber von *Ceratodus forsteri*, zugleich ein Beitrag zur vergleichenden Histologie der Fischleber. SEMON's Zoologische Forschungsreisen, I, p. 333—375.

1900a BOULENGER, G. A., Exhibition of one of the type specimens of a new species of *Protopterus* from the Congo. Proc. Zool. Soc. London, 1900, p. 775.

1900b BOULENGER, G. A., Matériaux pour la Faune du Congo. (*Protopterus dolloi*.) Ann. Mus. Congo, Sér. 1, Zool., I, p. 129—164.

1901 BOULENGER, G. A., On a small Collection of Fishes from Lake Victoria made by order of Sir H. H. JOHNSTON, K. C. B. Proc. Zool. Soc. London, 1901, II, p. 158.

1902 BOULENGER, G. A., Second Account of the Fishes collected by Dr. W. J. ANSORGE in the Niger Delta. Proc. Zool. Soc. London, 1902, II, p. 325.

1901 BRAUS, H., Die Muskeln und Nerven der *Ceratodus*-Flosse. SEMON's Zoologische Forschungsreisen, I, p. 139—300.

1904 BRAUS, H., Tatsächliches an der Entwicklung des Extremitätenskelettes bei den niedersten Formen. Zugleich ein Beitrag zur Entwicklungsgeschichte des Skelettes der Pinnae und der Visceralbögen. HARTWIG's Festschrift, p. 377—435.

1904 BRIDGE, T. W., "Fishes" in "Cambridge Natural History", VII, p. 139—537.

1908 BRINDLEY, H. H., Note on some Abnormalities of the Limbs and Tail of Dipnoan Fishes. Proc. Camb. Phil. Soc., X, p. 325—327.

1905 BROMAN, I., Ueber die Entwicklung der Mesenterien, der Leberligamente und der Leberform bei den Lungfischen. SEMON's Zoologische Forschungsreisen, I, p. 585—610.

1908 BRYCE, T. H., The dividing Cells of the Embryo of *Lepidosiren*. Journ. Anat. Physiol., XXXVIII, p. 70.

1904 BRYCE, T. H., The Histology of the Blood of the larva of *Lepidosiren paradoxa*. Pt. I. Structure of the Resting and Dividing Corpuscles. Trans. R. Soc. Edinb., XLI, p. 291—310.

1905 BRYCE, T. H., The Histology of the Blood of the Larva of *Lepidosiren paradoxa*. Pt. II. Haematogenesis. Trans. R. Soc. Edinb., XLI, p. 435—467. (Abstr. Lancet, CLXVII, p. 406.)
1905 BRYCE, T. H., Note on the development of the Thymus gland in *Lepidosiren paradoxa*. Journ. Anat. Physiol., XL, p. 91—99.
1901 BUDGETT, J. S., On the Breeding Habits of some West African Fishes, with an Account of the External Features in the Development of *Protopterus annectens* and a Description of the Larva of *Polypterus lapradei*. Trans. Zool. Soc. London, XVI, p. 115—136. (Abstr. in Zool. Centralbl., IX, p. 93—95.)
1900 BURCKHARDT, R., Das Zentralnervensystem von *Ceratodus forsteri*. C. R. Congr. internat. Zool. Berne, p. 314—315.
1901 DEAN, BASHFORD, Palaeontological Notes. Mem. New York Acad. Sci., II, p. 87—123.
1903 DEAN, BASHFORD, Obituary Notice of a Lung-Fish. Popular Science Monthly, p. 33—39.
1904 DEAN, BASHFORD, Still another Memoir on *Palaeospondylus*. Science, (2) XIX, p. 425, 426.
1906 DEAN, BASHFORD, Notes on the living specimens of the Australian Lung-Fish, *Ceratodus forsteri*, in the Zoological Society's Collection. Proc. Zool. Soc. London, 1906, I, p. 168—178.
1907 DEAN, BASHFORD, Dr. EASTMAN's Recent Papers on the Kinship of Arthrodires. Science, (2) XXVI, p. 46—50.
1908 DEAN, BASHFORD, Studies on Fossil Fishes during the year 1907. Science, (2) XXVII, p. 201—205.
1909 DEAN, BASHFORD, Studies on Fossil Fishes (Sharks, Chimaeroids and Arthrodires). Mem. Amer. Mus. Nat. Hist., IX, p. 5.
1906 DOLLO, L., Sur quelques points d'ethologie paléontologiques relatifs aux Poissons. Bull. Soc. belge de Géologie, de Paléontologie et d'Hydrologie (Bruxelles), XX.
1907 DOLLO, L., "Les Psychodontes sont des Arthrodires". Bull. Soc. belge de Géologie, de Paléontologie et d'Hydrologie (Bruxelles), XXI.
1901 EASTMAN, C. R., Review of BASHFORD DEAN's "Palaeontological Notes". Amer. Naturalist, XXXV, p. 418—420.
1902 EASTMAN, C. R., Some hitherto unpublished observations of ORESTES ST. JOHN on Palaeozoic Fishes. Amer. Naturalist, XXXVI, No. 428.
1903 EASTMAN, C. R., Carboniferous Fishes from the Central Western States. Bull. Mus. Comp. Zool. Harvard, XXXIX, p. 188.
1904 EASTMAN, C. R., A peculiar modification amongst Permian Dipnoans. Amer. Naturalist, XXXVII, p. 493—495.
1906a EASTMAN, C. R., Structure and Relations of *Mylostoma*. Bull. Mus. Comp. Zool. Harvard, L, p. 1—30.
1906b EASTMAN, C. R., Dipnoan Affinities of Arthrodires. Amer. Journ. Science, (4) XXI, p. 131—143.
1907a EASTMAN, C. R., Mylostomid Dentition. Bull. Mus. Comp. Zool. Harvard, L, p. 211—228.
1907b EASTMAN, C. R., The Devonic Fishes of the New York Formation. New York State Education Department, N. Y. State Museum, Albany.
1908 EASTMAN, C. R., The Devonian Fishes of Iowa. Iowa Geol. Survey, XVIII, p. 29—344.
1906 ETHERIDGE, R., The Cranial Buckler of a Dipnoan Fish, probably *Ganorhynchus*, from the Devonian Beds of the Murrumbidgee River, New South Wales. Rec. Austral. Mus., VI, p. 129—132.
1904 FRAAS, E., *Ceratodus priscus* E. FRAAS aus dem Hauptbuntsandstein. Ber. Oberrhein. Geol. Ver., XXXVII, p. 30—32.
1904a FÜRBRINGER, K., Beiträge zur Morphologie des Skeletes der Dipnoer, nebst Bemerkungen über Pleuracanthiden, Holocephalen und Squaliden. SEMON's Zoologische Forschungsreisen, I, p. 423—510.
1904b FÜRBRINGER, K., Notiz über einige Beobachtungen am Dipnoerkopf. Anat. Anzeiger, XXIV, p. 405—408.
1906 GIACOMINI, ERCOLE, Sulle capsule surrenali e sul simpatico dei Dipnoi. Ricerche in *Protopterus annectens*. Nota prelim. Rend. Accad. Lincei (5), XV, 1. sem., p. 394—398.
1901 GOEPPERT, E., Der Kehlkopf von *Protopterus annectens* (OWEN). Anatomische Untersuchung. HAECKEL's Festschrift, p. 115—132.
1903 GOODRICH, E. S., On the Dermal Fin-rays of Fishes. Quart. Journ. Micr. Sci., XLVII, p. 465—522.
1907 GOODRICH, E. S., On the Scales of Fish, Living and Extinct, and their Importance in Classification. Proc. Zool. Soc. London, p. 751—774.
1909 GOODRICH, E. S., Vertebrata Craniata (First Fascicle, Cyclostomes and Fishes) in "Treatise on Zoology", edited by Sir RAY LANKESTER, K. C. B., London.
1904 GREGORY, E. H., The Relations of the Anterior Visceral Arches to the Cranium. Biol. Bulletin, VII, p. 55—69.
1905 GREGORY, E. H., Die Entwicklung der Kopfhöhlen und des Kopfmesoderms bei *Ceratodus forsteri*. SEMON's Zoologische Forschungsreisen, I, p. 610, 661.
1906 GREIL, A., Ueber die Entstehung der Kiemenderivate von *Ceratodus*. Anat. Anzeiger, Erg.-Heft, p. 115—131.
1908 GREIL, A., Entwicklungsgeschichte des Kopfes und des Blutgefässystems von *Ceratodus forsteri*. Erster Teil. Gesamtentwicklung bis zum Beginn der Blutzirkulation. SEMON's Zoologische Forschungsreisen, I, p. 661—934.
1901 HALKETT, A., An African Dipnoid Fish (*Protopterus annectens*). Ottawa Naturalist, XIV, p. 184—187.
1904 HAUG, E., Sur la Faune de couches à *Ceratodus* du Djoua, près Timassinine (Sahara). C. R. Acad. Science, CXXXVIII, p. 1529—1531.

1901 Hotch, Das Sehorgan von *Protopterus annectens*. Arch. mikr. Anat., LXIV, p. 90—110.
1901 v. Huene, F., *Rhynchotus emigratus* v. Huene. Centralbl. f. Mineral., p. 179.
1905a Hussakof, L., Notes on the Devonian Placoderm *Dinichthys intermedius* Newb. Bull. Amer. Mus. Nat. Hist., XXI, Art. IV, p. 27—36.
1905b Hussakof, L., On the structure of two imperfectly known Dinichthyids. Bull. Amer. Mus. Nat. Hist., XXI, Art. XXV, p. 409—418.
1906 Hussakof, L., Studies on the Arthrodira. Mem. Amer. Mus. Nat. Hist., IX, p. 103—154.
1908a Hussakof, L., Catalogue of the Type and Figured Specimens of Fossil Vertebrata in the American Museum of Natural History. Part I. Fishes. Bull. Amer. Mus. Nat. Hist., June 1908.
1908b Hussakof, L., Review of Eastman's "Devonic Fishes of the New York Formations". Science, (2) XXVIII, p. 311—313.
1901 Hussakof, L., The Systematic Relationship of certain American Arthrodires. Bull. Amer. Mus. Nat. Hist., XXVI, Art. XX, p. 263—272.
1902 Jaekel, O., Ueber *Coccosteus* und die Beurteilung der Placodermen. Sitzungsber. Gesellsch. naturf. Freunde Berlin, p. 103—105.
1903a Jaekel, O., Ueber die Organisation und systematische Stellung der Asterolepiden. Zeitschr. deutsch. geolog. Gesellsch., Mai-Protokoll, LV, p. 41—60.
1903b Jaekel, O., Ueber die Epiphyse und Hypophyse. Sitzungsber. Gesellsch. naturf. Freunde Berlin, p. 27—58.
1904 Jaekel, O., Neue Wirbeltierfunde im Oberdevon von Wildungen. September-Protokoll der deutschen geol. Gesellsch., LVI, p. 159—164.
1906a Jaekel, O., Ueber die Mundbildung der Wirbeltiere. Sitzungsber. Gesellsch. naturf. Freunde Berlin, p. 7—32.
1906b Jaekel, O., Einige Beiträge zur Morphologie der ältesten Wirbeltiere. Sitzungsber. Gesellsch. naturf. Freunde Berlin, p. 180, 189.
1906c Jaekel, O., Neue Wirbeltierfunde aus dem Devon von Wildungen. Sitzungsber. Gesellsch. naturf. Freunde Berlin, p. 73—85.
1907 Jaekel, O., Ueber *Pholidostens* nov. gen., die Mundbildung und die Körperform der Placodermen. Sitzungsber. Gesellsch. naturf. Freunde Berlin, p. 3—19.
1896a Kellicott, W. E., The Development of the Vascular System of *Ceratodus*. Anat. Anzeiger, XXVI, p. 200—208. (Correction p. 400.)
1896b Kellicott, W. E., The development of the vascular and respiratory systems of *Ceratodus*. Mem. New York Acad., II, p. 135—249.
1897a Kerr, J. Graham, Remarks upon his recent Expedition to Paraguay in quest of *Lepidosiren*. Proc. Zool. Soc. London, p. 921—923.
1897b Kerr, J. Graham, The *Lepidosiren* of South America. Nat. Science, XII, p. 3.
1897c Kerr, J. Graham, On the Development of *Lepidosiren*. Proc. Zool. Soc. London, p. 921.
1898a Kerr, J. Graham, On the dry season habits of *Lepidosiren*. Letter from R. J. Hunt. Proc. Zool. Soc. London, 1898, p. 41—44.
1898b Kerr, J. Graham, Exhibition of *Lepidosiren* and accompanying Teleosts. Proc. Zool. Soc. London, p. 492.
1899a Kerr, J. Graham, The External Features in the Development of *Lepidosiren paradoxa* Fitz. Proc. Roy. Soc., LXV, p. 160, 161 (also in Zool. Anzeiger, XXII).
1899b Kerr, J. Graham, Development of *Lepidosiren*. Abstr. Nat. Science, XIV, p. 432, 433.
1900a Kerr, J. Graham, The External Features in the Development of *Lepidosiren paradoxa* Fitz. Phil. Trans. Roy. Soc., B CXCII, p. 299—330.
1900b Kerr, J. Graham, Note on Hypotheses as to the Origin of the paired Limbs of Vertebrates. Proc. Camb. Phil. Soc., X, p. 227—235.
1900c Kerr, J. Graham, The Zoological Position of *Palaeospondylus* Traquair. Proc. Camb. Phil. Soc., X, p. 298 and 299.
1901a Kerr, J. Graham, The Development of *Lepidosiren paradoxa*. Pt. II. With a Note upon Corresponding Stages in the Development of *Protopterus annectens*. Quart. Journ. Micr. Science, (2) XLV, p. 1—40. (Abstr. in Zool. Centralbl., IX, p. 143—146.)
1901b Kerr, J. Graham, On the male Genito-urinary Organs of *Lepidosiren* and *Protopterus*. Proc. Zool. Soc. London, 1901, p. 484—496. (Abstr. in Zool. Anzeiger, XXV, p. 30—31.)
1901c Kerr, J. Graham, The Genito-urinary Organs of Dipnoan Fishes. Proc. Camb. Phil. Soc., XI, p. 329—333.
1901d Kerr, J. Graham, The Development of *Lepidosiren paradoxa*. Pt. III. Development of the Skin and its Derivatives. Quart. Journ. Micr. Science, XLVI, p. 417—459.
1901e Kerr, J. Graham, The Origin of the Paired Limbs of Vertebrates. Rep. Brit. Association for the Advancement of Science, 1901. (Abstr. in Nature, LXIV, p. 588—589.)

1902 Kerr, J. Graham, The Early Development of Muscles and Motor Nerves in *Lepidosiren*. Rep. Brit. Association for the Advancement of Science, p. 655—657.
1904 Kerr, J. Graham, On some Points in the Early Development of Motor Nerve trunks and Myotomes in *Lepidosiren paradoxa* (Fitz.). Trans. Roy. Soc. Edinb., XLI, p. 119—127.
1906 Kerr, J. Graham, The Embryology of certain of the Lower Fishes, and its Bearing upon Vertebrate Morphology. Proc. Roy. Phys. Soc. Edinb., XVI, p. 191—215.
1907a Kerr, J. Graham, Note on the Cause of Disappearance of the Fifth Aortic Arch in Air-breathing Vertebrates. Proc. Roy. Phys. Soc. Edinb., XVII, p. 167, 168.
1907b Kerr, J. Graham, Note on the Autostylic Skull of Vertebrates. Proc. Roy. Phys. Soc. Edinb., XVII, p. 169.
1908 Kerr, J. Graham, Note on Swim-bladder and Lungs. Proc. Roy. Phys. Soc. Edinb., XVII, p. 170—174.
1910 Kerr, J. Graham, Development of the Alimentary Canal and its Appendages in *Lepidosiren* and *Protopterus*. Quart. Journ. Micr. Science. (In the Press.)
1906 Mercial, G., *Lepidosiren paradoxa* Fitz. Riv. Ital. Sc. nat. Siena, XXVI, p. 59—61.
1902 Moore, J. E. S., The Tanganyika Problem, London 1902, p. 152. (Fig. of *Protopterus aethiopicus*.)
1906 Murray, J. A., Zahl und Größenverhältnisse der Chromosomen bei *Lepidosiren paradoxa* Fitz. Anat. Anzeiger, XXIX, p. 203—206.
1903 Neumayr, L., Die Entwicklung des Darmkanales von *Ceratodus forsteri*. Verh. anat. Ges., XVII, p. 139—142.
1904 Neumayr, L., Recherches sur le développement du foie du pancréas et de la rate chez *Ceratodus forsteri*. C. R. Ass. Anat. Sess. VI, p. 73—77.
1904 Neumayr, L., Die Entwicklung des Darmkanales, von Lunge, Leber, Milz und Pankreas bei *Ceratodus forsteri*. Semon's Zoologische Forschungsreisen, I, p. 377—422.
1904 Sabatier, A., Sur les mains scapulaires et pelviennes des Poissons holocéphales et chez les Dipneustes. C. R. Acad. Science, CXXXVIII, p. 249—252.
1895 Sarasin, F., Exhibit of *Protopterus annectens* which had just left its burrow. Arch. Science Nat., XX, p. 594, 595.
1894 Schulz, W. A., Ueberblick über die Geschichte der Auffindung von *Lepidosiren paradoxa* Fitz. Verh. k. k. zool.-bot. Ges. Wien, LIII, p. 588—591.
1893a Semon, R., Verbreitung, Lebensweise und Fortpflanzung des *Ceratodus forsteri*. Semon's Zoologische Forschungsreisen, I, p. 11—28.
1893b Semon, R., Die äußere Entwicklung des *Ceratodus forsteri*. Ibidem, I, p. 29—50.
1895 Semon, R., Vermeintliche "äußere" Kiemen bei *Ceratodus*-Embryonen. Anat. Anzeiger, X, p. 322—333.
1896 Semon, R., Im australischen Busch und an den Küsten des Korallenmeeres, Leipzig 1896.
1898 Semon, R., Die Entwickelung der paarigen Flossen des *Ceratodus forsteri*. Semon's Zoologische Forschungsreisen, I, p. 59—111.
1899a Semon, R., Weitere Beiträge zur Physiologie der Dipnoerflossen, auf Grund neuer, von Mr. Arthur Thompson an gedungenen Exemplaren von *Ceratodus* angestellten Beobachtungen. Zool. Anzeiger, XXII, p. 294—300.
1899b Semon, R., Ueber die Entwicklung der Zahngebilde der Dipnoer. Sitzungsber. d. Ges. f. Morphologie und Physiologie in München, XV, p. 75—85.
1901a Semon, R., Die Zahnentwicklung des *Ceratodus forsteri*. Semon's Zoologische Forschungsreisen, I, p. 113—135.
1901b Semon, R., Die Furchung und Entwicklung der Keimblätter bei *Ceratodus forsteri*. Ibidem, I, p. 301—332. (Abstr. in Zool. Centralbl., VIII, p. 781—782.)
1901c Semon, R., Zur Entwicklungsgeschichte des Urogenitalsystems der Dipnoer. Zool. Anzeiger, XXIV, p. 131—135.
1901d Semon, R., Die „ektodermale Medianzahl" des *Ceratodus forsteri*. Arch. f. Entwickl.-Mech., XI, p. 310—320. (Abstr. in Zool. Centralbl., VIII, p. 781—782.)
1901e Semon, R., Ueber das Verwandtschaftsverhältnis der Dipnoer und Amphibien. Zool. Anzeiger, XXIV, p. 180—188. (Abstr. in Journ. Roy. Micr. Soc., 1901, p. 403.)
1901f Semon, R., Normentafel zur Entwicklungsgeschichte des *Ceratodus forsteri*. Keibel, Normentafeln zur Entwicklungsgeschichte der Wirbeltiere, Heft 3.
1902 Severtzoff, A. N., Zur Entwicklungsgeschichte des *Ceratodus forsteri*. Anat. Anzeiger, XXI, p. 593—608.
1908 Smith, G. Elliot, The Cerebral Cortex in *Lepidosiren*, with comparative Notes on the Interpretation of certain Features of the Forebrain in other Vertebrates. Anat. Anzeiger, XXXIII, p. 513—540.
1890 Sollas, W. J. and L. B. J., An Account of the Devonian Fish *Palaeospondylus gunni* Traquair. Phil. Trans. Roy. Soc., B CXLVI, p. 267—294. (Abstr. in Proc. Roy. Soc., LXXII, p. 98, 99.)
1901 Spengel, J. W., Ueber Schwimmblasen, Lungen und Kiementaschen der Wirbeltiere. Zool. Jahrbücher, Suppl. VII, p. 727—749.
1895 Tagliani, G., Le fibre de Mauthner nel midollo spinale dei Vertebrati inferiori (anamni). Arch. Zool. Ital., II, p. 383—428.

1900   Traquair, R. H., Presidential Address to the Zoological Section. Rep. Brit. Association for the Advancement of Science, 1900.
1903a Traquair, R. H., On the Distribution of Fossil Fish-remains in the Carboniferous Rocks of the Edinburgh District. Trans. Roy. Soc. Edinb., XL, p. 687—706.
1903b Traquair, R. H., The Lower Devonian Fishes of Gemünden. Trans. Roy. Soc. Edinb., XL, p. 723—739.
1908   Traquair, R. H., On Fossil Fish-remains from the Old Red Sandstone of Shetland. Trans. Roy. Soc. Edinb. XLVI, p. 321—329.
1908   Whiteaves, J. F., Illustrations of the Fossil Fishes of the Devonian Rocks of Canada. Pt. III, Supplementary Notes. Trans. Roy. Soc. Canada, 3. Series, 1907—1908, p. 245—275.
1903   Wiedersheim, R., Ueber den Kehlkopf der Ganoiden und Dipnoer. Anat. Anzeiger, XXII, p. 522—535.
1904a Wiedersheim, R., Ueber das Vorkommen eines Kehlkopfes bei Ganoiden und Dipnoern, sowie über die Phylogenie der Lunge. Zool. Jahrbücher, Suppl. VII, p. 1—66.
1904b Wiedersheim, R., Nachträgliche Bemerkungen zu meinem Aufsatz über den Kehlkopf der Ganoiden und Dipnoer. Anat. Anzeiger, XXIV, p. 651—652.
1901a Wilson, Gregg, The First Foundation of the Lung of *Ceratodus*. (Preliminary Notice.) Proc. Roy. Phys. Soc. Edinb., XIV, p. 319—321. (Abstr. in Journ. Roy. Micr. Soc., 1901, p. 510—511.)
1901b Wilson, Gregg, Embryonic Excretory Organs of *Ceratodus*. (Preliminary Notice.) Ibidem, p. 321—323. (Abstr. in Journ. Roy. Micr. Soc., p. 540—541.)
1906a Woodward, A. S., On a Tooth of *Ceratodus* and a Dinosaurian Claw from the Lower Jurassic of Victoria, Australia. Ann. Mag. Nat. Hist., XVIII, p. 1—3.
1906b Woodward, A. S., On a Carboniferous Fish Fauna from the Mansfield District, Victoria. Mem. Nat. Mus. Melbourne, I, p. 1—32.

Frommannsche Buchdruckerei (Hermann Pohle) in Jena. — 1905

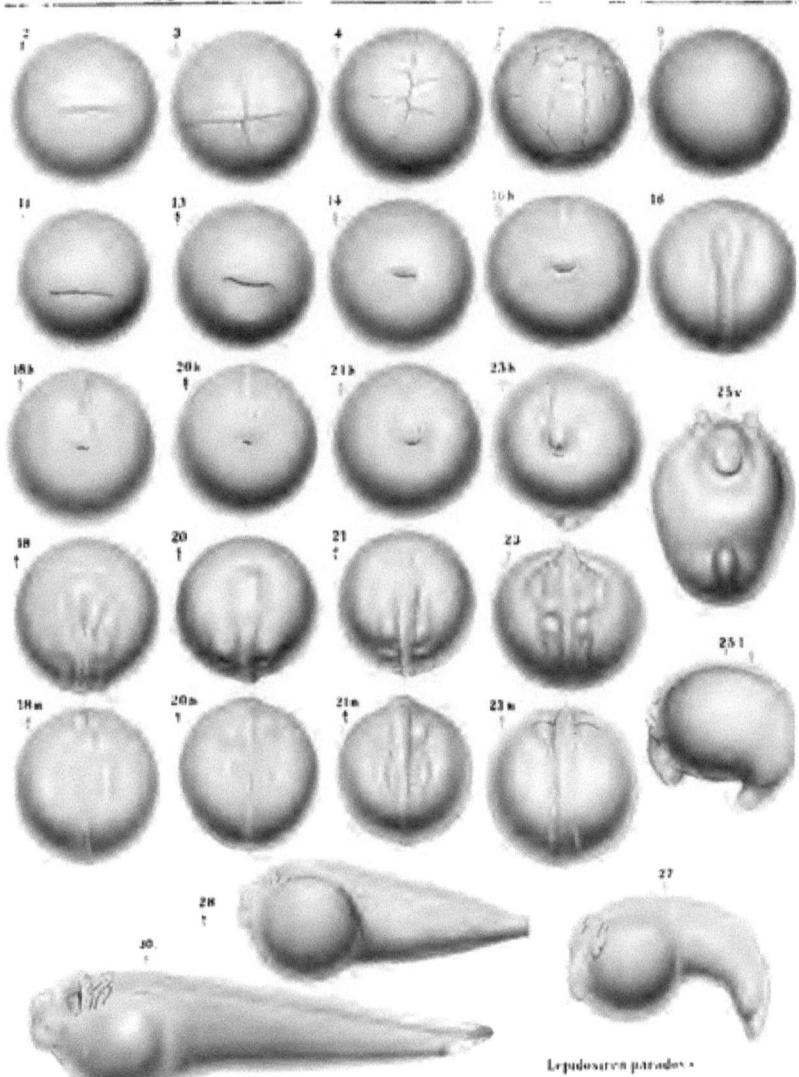

Lepidosiren paradoxa

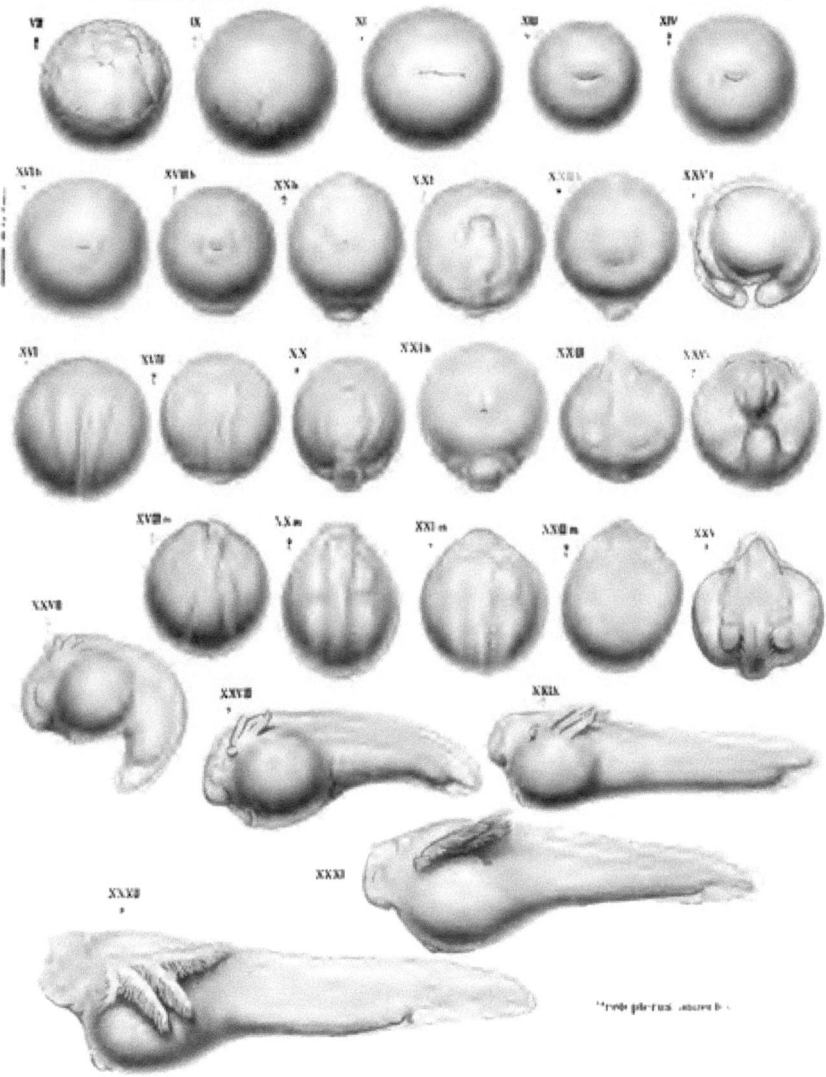

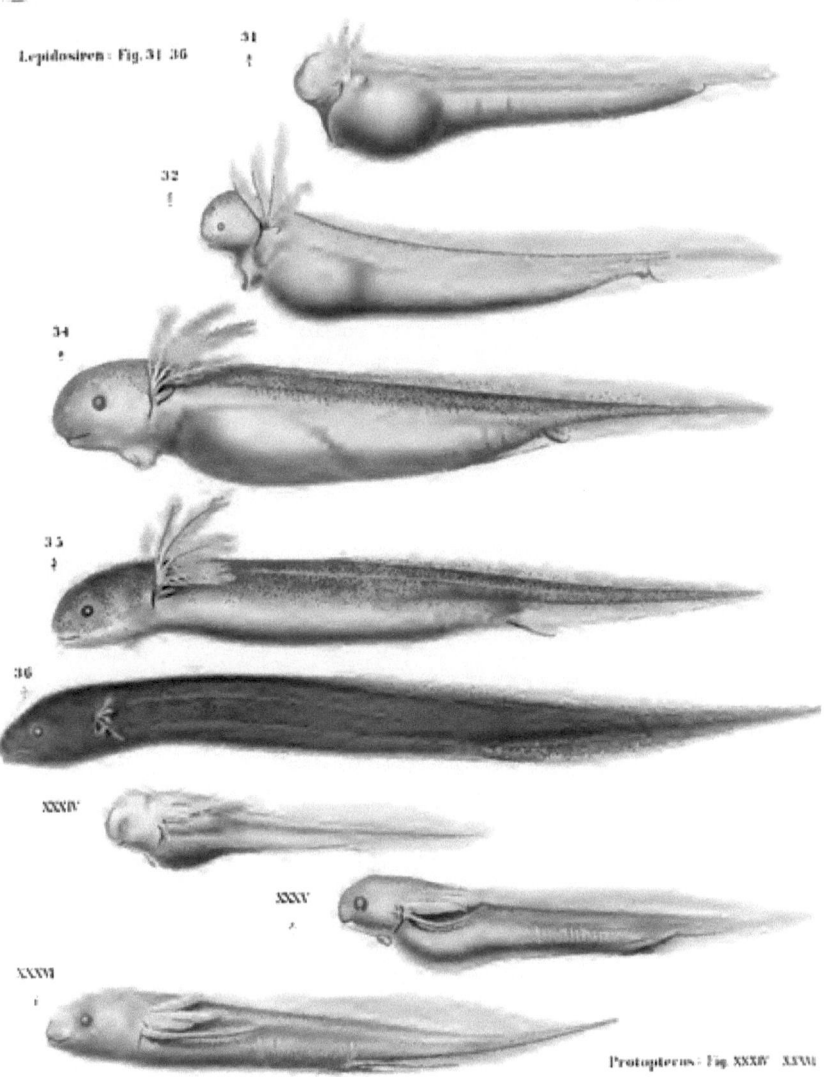